SCOOBY-DOO!™

and the Truth Behind

SEA MONSTERS

BY TERRY COLLINS

ILLUSTRATED BY DARIO BRIZUELA

raintree

a Capstone company — publishers for children

Raintree is an imprint of Capstone Global Library Limited, a
company incorporated in England and Wales having its
registered office at 7 Pilgrim Street, London, EC4V 6LB —
Registered company number: 6695582

www.raintree.co.uk
myorders@raintree.co.uk

Editorial Credits:
Editor: Shelly Lyons
Designer: Ted Williams
Art Director: Nathan Gassman
Production Specialist: Tori Abraham

ISBN 978-1-4062-8898-8 (paperback)
18 17 16 15 14
10 9 8 7 6 5 4 3 2 1

British Library Cataloguing in Publication Da
A full catalogue record for this book is available

Acknowledgements
We would like to thank the following for permiss
Design Elements: Shutterstock: ailin1, AllAnd, hug

The illustrations in this book were created tradit

We would like to thank Elizabeth Tucker Gould, Professor of English, Binghamton
University for her invaluable help in the preparation of this book.

Every effort has been made to contact copyright holders of material reproduced
in this book. Any omissions will be rectified in subsequent printings if notice is
given to the publisher.

All the internet addresses (URLs) given in this book were valid at
the time of going to press. However, due to the dynamic nature
of the internet, some addresses may have changed, or sites
may have changed or ceased to exist since publication. While
the author and publisher regret any inconvenience this may
cause readers, no responsibility for any such changes can be
accepted by either the author or the publisher.

Printed and bound in China.

The weather at the beach was beautiful. Velma opened the cool box. "Lunch time, gang!" she shouted. "Hey, where's Scooby?"

"No sign of him here!" Shaggy replied.

"He's not on the beach," Fred said.

"Scooby-Doo, where are you?" Daphne called towards the sea.

"Rover here!" Scooby cried.

"Like, you totally crushed my castle, Scoob," said Shaggy.

Scooby pointed towards the water. "Rea ronster!" he yelled.

"So how big can sea monsters get, anyway?" Shaggy wondered.

"Well, the Leviathan is one of the biggest sea creatures of legend," said Fred. "One report estimated he was 1,448 kilometres (900 miles) long!"

"I'm sorry I asked," Shaggy said.

"He had rows of sharp teeth," Fred continued, "and breathed fire."

"Yikes!" said Scooby.

"So what's the most famous sea monster?" Shaggy asked.

"That's easy," replied Daphne. "The Loch Ness monster, or Nessie."

"Ressie?" asked Scooby.

Nessie has a small head and a long neck. She also has at least one hump on her back. Tourists from all around the world travel to Loch Ness in Scotland to try and see her. But Nessie has never been caught. Most people think she's a myth.

"So, have sea monsters ever attacked people?" Shaggy asked.

"Some of them, yes," Velma replied. "The mythical kraken was probably a type of giant squid that still exists today. The kraken is supposed to have lived off the coasts of Norway and Greenland. It is thought to have been about 15 metres (50 feet) long."

"Rig rea ronster!" Scooby said.

"Very big," said Fred. "With eight long arms, it was said to be able to easily grab ships and pull them under water."

YIKES!

Are there any other well known sea monsters?

There's Ogopogo. It is thought to live in Lake Okanagan in Canada. Ogopogo is thought to be able to swim as fast as 64 kilometres (40 miles) an hour.

"Yes," said Velma. "It is believed to live in and around the Congo River in Africa."

"No one has ever taken a picture or found any proof that the monster exists," Fred added. "But experts think it could be a long-lost dinosaur."

"It's said to have the body of an elephant and a long, flexible neck and tail," said Velma.

"According to the crew of the *Kuranda*, yes!" Velma said. "In 1973 a giant jellyfish got stuck to the front of their ship."

"How big was it?" Shaggy wondered.

"It weighed about 18 metric tons," said Velma, as she showed the gang the screen of her tablet. "The tentacles were more than 61 metres (200 ft) long."

"What should I do if I see a sea monster?" Shaggy asked.

"If you can, take pictures or a video of what you see," Daphne replied.

"Yes," said Fred, "and try to get a good shot. The pictures people have taken of the Loch Ness monster are blurry and dark."

GLOSSARY

legend old story handed down from the past

myth story told by people in ancient times; myths often tried to explain natural events

mythical imaginary; only found in myths

squid sea animal with a long, soft body and 10 finger-like arms used to grasp food

tentacle long, flexible limb used for moving, feeling and grabbing

venom poisonous liquid produced by some animals

BOOKS

Sea Monsters (Legends of the Sea), Catherine Veitch (Raintree, 2010)

Spectacular Squid (Creatures of the Deep), Casey Rand (Raintree, 2012)

INDEX

WEBSITES

www.bbc.co.uk/sn/prehistoric_life/ dinosaurs/seamonsters/
Discover amazing facts, have a look at realistic computer-generated images and even play a sea monster game.

www.nationalgeographic.com/ seamonsters/index.html
Go on a prehistoric adventure through time and learn about monsters of the sea from all over the world through facts, photos and video clips.